REVELATION

VISIONS OF VICTORY

Ian A. Fair

STREAMS of MERCY
study series

Revelation: Visions of Victory

HillCrest
PUBLISHING

1648 Campus Ct.
Abilene, TX 79601
www.hillcrestpublishing.com

Cover Design and Typesetting by Sarah Bales

Copyright © 2000

Ian A. Fair

Scripture quotations unless otherwise designated, are from The Holy Bible, New International Version, copyright © 1973, 1978, 1984 by International Bible Society. Used by permission of Zondervan Bible Publishers.

Printed in the United States of America

ISBN 0-89112-280-X

1,2,3,4,5

TABLE OF CONTENTS

FOR TEACHERS AND CLASS LEADERS...

The word of God is powerful. This belief is the driving force behind the Streams of Mercy Study Series. Assigned reading, brief commentary, and questions for reflection and class discussion are presented for each section of the biblical book. The goal is changed lives–changed by the power of the Word.

Consider the following suggestions as you prepare for class:

- Even though class members may have read the passage assigned for the week, select some verses to be read aloud in class: let the Word speak.

- Give a brief summary of the points made in the lesson, then begin working with the questions. As you prepare for your class, explore the possibility of a variety of answers to the questions. Don't be afraid of momentary silence when you ask the questions; give people a chance to think, but be prepared to prompt the discussion.

- Be creative with your classroom time. Sometimes, have the class work in small groups to discuss the questions. Consider having someone prepare to comment on a particular question for the next scheduled class meeting. Perhaps, you could ask someone to be prepared to share his or her experience with finding time to work on the lesson in the middle of work and family obligations–in this way we acknowledge the struggle to make time for Bible study. Give someone the task of praying for the whole class throughout the coming week as they all find time for study. Let the class know this will be happening.

- Ask class members to make a plan of action that puts into practice the things the text calls for. This may be a service project or a commitment to pray for help in overcoming specific problems the text brings to light. Be prepared to suggest plans of action and to get the class involved in brainstorming about this. Avoid taking charge too much, let the class get involved.

- Find out if anyone in the class would like to create banners or any kind of visuals pertaining to the study. This is a good way to validate the gifts of others.

- Try to inspire excitement about the class working together each week to hear and understand the word of God. Stress that this is one of the ways we are in fellowship with one another.

- Be sensitive to people who don't want to speak in class. Encourage those who want to speak, but who may be a little tentative. Practice good leadership by not allowing any one person to dominate the discussions.

- Try to keep the discussions on target. One complaint we often hear about Bible classes is that the group too easily gets off the subject. These volumes are designed to promote discussion of the biblical text. Pray for help to keep the class focused without preventing healthy discussion.

Nothing is more important than seeking God's guidance as you prepare for class. Ask him to open your heart so the text speaks to you and convicts you, then you will be more prepared to lead the group. May the Lord bless all of you as you seek his will, and may you know the everflowing streams of his mercy.

The Editors

INTRODUCTION

A Mysterious Book!

A t first glance Revelation is a strange and mysterious book! Its language is like no other book in the New Testament. Revelation speaks in a highly figurative, symbolic, dramatic, and idiomatic manner in which God reveals matters of urgent significance to Christians facing enormous trials. What complicates our understanding and appreciation of this great book is the fact that more speculative theology has surrounded the figurative language of Revelation than any other book in the Bible. Furthermore, to many, Revelation is a somewhat frightening or threatening book that focuses on end of the world battles, tribulations, and judgments. Whenever some skirmish breaks out in the middle east we hear warnings concerning the signs of the times, the battle of Armageddon, and the end of the world.

Final end of the

world battles

are not what this

great book

is all about!

Unfortunately, these concerns spring from extremely speculative approaches to Revelation and not from the text itself. The strange language and cosmic visions we encounter in Revelation are a fertile breeding ground for such thinking. However, final end of the world battles are not what this great book is all about! John informs us in the first paragraph of Revelation that this message concerns things that were to "take place soon" and that the times of these things was "at hand" (1:2-3). Whatever the strange visions might be, and however one is to understand the figurative language of Revelation, John clearly explains that Revelation concerns things that would soon break out in the life of the churches to whom it was addressed towards the close of the first century A.D.

How Does Revelation Speak to Us?

Revelation is a letter to seven churches of Asia (Rev 1:11) that draws heavily on the Old Testament and other writings of the Jewish-Christian community. One should not attempt to read Revelation literally, but should seek to understand the figurative use of the Old Testament and the symbolic idiom used by John. Much of Jewish Christian literature is couched in poetic and symbolic language for dramatic effect. The student of Scripture should realize that truth is often conveyed in poetic and figurative language (Psalms, Proverbs, Parables, etc.), and should not confuse figurative language with fables and fiction which might have little or no relationship to truth.

The Author and Date of Revelation

The author describes himself simply as John. The early church believed this to be the Apostle John, but this has not been universally accepted. The author could possibly be some other respected person in the church in Asia in the 1st century whose name was John. We have no final information on the authorship of Revelation other than the testimony of the early church and the reference to John in 1:1, 9. The author must have been a highly regarded and respected member of the church for God to single him out for this daunting task and for the book to have been so readily accepted.

Most scholars today prefer the date of AD 96 and the reign of Emperor Domitian for the writing of Revelation. The historical and sociological circumstances of the church reflected in Revelation relate best to this date.

The Seven Churches

Revelation was a unique circular letter written by God and Jesus to seven churches in Asia (now modern Turkey). Revelation 1:1, 4, 11 and chapters 2 and 3 clearly establish this. We know that there were more than seven churches in Asia in the first century, but the figurative number of seven, which dominates Revelation and symbolically signifies completeness, implies that the letter was in fact written to all of the churches in Asia. These churches were about to experience a severe crisis of hostility and persecution from their Jewish, Roman, and Pagan neighbors, and John's vision calls them to an uncompromising faith in Jesus under all circumstances, even if this faithfulness to Jesus resulted in martyrdom (Rev 1:9).

The Structure of Revelation

Revelation is in the form of a two part drama with the high point coming in 12-14. The following structure demonstrates the ascending and descending nature of Revelation. Technically, we refer to this unique structure as a chiastic structure. This form of writing was common to both the Old and New Testaments. Revelation 1 11 is part one of the drama, chapters 12-22, are part two. Part one is more generic; Satan and Evil verses God. Part two focuses more attention on Satan, Rome, and the church. The final message of Revelation is that Satan uses nations to carry out his evil attacks on God's purpose, but in the end through Jesus' victory on the cross, God and his church triumph over Satan and his attacks. God's eternal purpose for his creation meets its decisive victory over Satan in Jesus Christ.

Prologue. 1:1-20

I. God's Imperfect Church   2:1-3:22
    Seven Letters to the Seven Churches

II. Is God in Control?   4:1-8:6
    Seven Seals on the Scroll

III. The Warning Judgments   8:1-11:19
     Seven Trumpets

IV. The Lamb - God's Answer to Evil   12:1-14:20
    Messages of God's Mercy

The Theological Message of Revelation

Revelation is a book about conquering Satan and his agents (overcoming in the NIV is not the best translation of this word). This theme is found in each of the seven letters in Revelation (2:7, 11, 17, 26; 3:5, 12, 21). The theology is that Christians who will not compromise their faith in Jesus even in the face of martyrdom and death, will through their martyrdom be victorious over Satan. The apex in Revelation comes in Rev 12:10, 11. The saints have conquered Satan through the blood of Jesus and their faithfulness to him. Salvation and victory belong to God. This is an important passage for Revelation. Please read it now! The theme of Revelation can therefore be summarized in one word, Victory!

The Continuing Relevance of Revelation

Christians today may not have to die as martyrs, but all will face crises in their lives and temptations from contemporary society to compromise their faith in Jesus. Jesus promises that through our faith in him and by resisting these temptations he will transform these crises into magnificent victories.

✢ Reflection and Application

1. From what you have learned about Revelation in this lesson, what is Revelation really about? Refer to 1:1-3 and 12:10,11.

2. What is it about Revelation that causes people to neglect it or pay such little attention to it? What do your friends normally think of Revelation?

3. How does one account for the strange language and idiom of Revelation (where does it come from?), and how does one work through this? What is the background to much of the confusion that exists regarding Revelation today?

4. How does attempting to understand the date of Revelation assist us in understanding the message of the book and applying it to our contemporary situation?

5. How would a knowledge of the nature of the seven churches in Asia assist us in understanding Revelation? What was the central message to the seven churches? (Refer to Revelation 2, 3).

6. Discuss the literary characteristics of Revelation in regard to drama and structure. How does a chiastic structure lead us to the core message or theme?

7. In your own words describe the theology or theme of Revelation. Refer to 2:7, 11, 17, 26; 3:5, 12, 21, and 12:10,11.

2
THE PROLOGUE

REV 1:1-20

The Structure of the Prologue

John's unique structure of Revelation involves bracketing the message of Revelation between a Prologue and an Epilogue (see the Structural Outline in Lesson 1). These two sections form "bookends" which define and limit what the revelation is all about. Much of what is introduced in the Prologue is repeated again in some form in the Epilogue, stressing and defining the importance and urgency of the message. Notice the parallels:

PROLOGUE	EPILOGUE
1:2	22:6
"...What must soon take place..."	"...what must soon take place..."
1:3	22:7
Blessing on the one who keeps the prophecy	Blessing on the one who keeps the prophecy

The intention of this literary device of Prologue-Epilogue is obviously to define the timetable for the events about to break in on the churches of Asia (soon), and to stress the urgency of the revelation (the churches were to constantly read, hear, and keep the words of the prophecy).

Source, Time, and Urgency – 1:1-3

The prologue opens in striking manner with a paragraph which stresses the Source of the revelation – it comes directly from God who speaks through Jesus and angels to John. This opening paragraph emphasizes the gravity and seriousness of the message contained in the revelation.

These first verses also clarify the time setting for the events of Revelation. Revelation does not concern events that will take place at the end of the world, or immediately prior to the end of the world as modern Premillennialists and

Dispensationalists claim. Revelation addresses the immediacy of what will soon take place and impact the lives of the churches in Asia in the first century. Driving this point home decisively, John maintains that the time of these things is near! The unique construction of this phrase in the original language implies that the significant time, or crisis time is about to break in on them, in fact, it is already brooding over them, hence the urgency of the revelation. John emphasizes this fact by observing that the revelation he is writing reflects the visions (even to all that he saw, 1:2) that he has only recently seen on Patmos (1:9).

Drawing attention still further to the urgency of the crisis about to impact the churches of Asia, God pronounces a blessing on those who read the revelation to the churches, and to those who hear and keep the message contained in the revelation. The RSV correctly translates this as "reads aloud the words of the prophecy," reflecting the practice of the early church of reading scripture aloud (most often the Old Testament) in the church assembly. The sense of the text, that this public reading, hearing, and keeping should be a regular feature in the life of the church in Asia at this time, adds to the urgency of the crises about to threaten the lives of the Asian churches.

The Salutation to the Seven Churches of Asia – 1:4-8
In typical Christian epistolary form John greets the seven churches with a blessing of grace (God's favor) and peace (spiritual prosperity and inner strength). This epistolary greeting had become standard practice in Christian letters (see similar greetings in each of Paul's letters). This blessing, John stresses, came directly from the eternal God (who is, and who was, and who is to come), from the all seeing Holy Spirit (the seven spirits), and from Jesus the faithful witness (martyr) of God. Jesus, the first-born of the dead, is the foundation of all future resurrections. He is the ruler over all kings of the earth, including the Roman Emperor. He is the one who loves the church and who has brought Christians into the reign of God as a kingdom of priests who through their martyrdom offer their lives as a sacrifice to God. Jesus, in addition to being the loving redeemer, will also come as sovereign Lord (to him be glory and dominion for ever) in final judgment, bringing God's righteous judgment (he is coming with the clouds) on all who oppose God and his people. Emphasizing the seriousness of the revelation, John closes this salutation with the magisterial statement by God himself (I am the Alpha and the Omega...the Almighty).

The Voice and the Vision – 1:9-20
Although on the surface Rev 1:9 seems to be a statement by John intended to comfort his audience, and it is such, this passage becomes thematic for the message and theology of Revelation. John emphasizes first that he, like the Christians in Asia, is experiencing tribulation. But this is nothing unique to John and the churches in Asia, for Jesus had likewise experienced adversity to the point of martyrdom. John's singular point, however, is not merely the mention of shared tribulation, rather, he seeks to demonstrate that tribulation, kingdom, and patient endurance are inextricably linked.

A pivotal theme in John's Revelation is that through patiently and faithfully endur-

11

ing tribulation (persecution) the saints will share in the reign (kingdom) of Jesus. John personalizes the thought of suffering tribulation by stating that he is on the island of Patmos (a penal colony for political prisoners) because of the message from God he has been proclaiming. We conclude from the context of Revelation that this message involved encouraging Christians not to venerate the Emperor as a divine ruler, but to worship only Jesus as their divine king – Jesus is Lord, not Caesar!

The intention of the vision is to present Jesus, not Caesar, in full divine glory as the true king of the nations.

On the Lord's day (Sunday, the day of the resurrection) John is told to write a book in the form of a letter to the seven churches of Asia. He immediately sees a vision of Jesus unlike any previously experienced. Jesus appears in divine regalia, a picture drawn from several Old Testament passages in Ezekiel, Daniel, Zechariah and others. The vision presents Jesus as the powerful and triumphant Son of Man of Daniel 7 who comes in judgment (he has a sharp two-edged sword in his mouth) over rebellious nations. The intention of the vision is to present Jesus, not Caesar, in full divine glory as the true king of the nations. Jesus then speaks, identifying himself clearly as the one in the vision, but in doing so adds that he is also the resurrected Christ who has ultimate control over Death (personified), the place of the dead (Hades), and in fact, the whole universe. Jesus then instructs John to write an account of the visions he had seen and how the visions would relate to what was about to break in on the Christians in Asia.

The final statement of Jesus reveals the mystery of the vision in which Jesus is seen holding seven stars in his right hand, and seven golden lampstands in the midst of which Jesus was standing. Lampstands (the Jewish Menorah) represent faithful witnesses (they shed the light of God). The seven churches, represented by the lampstands, are intended to be faithful witnesses to Jesus and God's plan. The seven stars are seven angels. Angels in the Jewish and biblical tradition are servants of God who do his bidding. It appears from Revelation and other Jewish-Christian writings of the period that angels were also some form of guardian angel, divine presence, or spiritual being responsible for God's creation. The main point for Revelation is that they represent the seven churches to whom Jesus is writing.

❧ Reflection and Application

1. What role do the Prologue and Epilogue play in the message of Revelation, and what do we learn about this message from the Prologue? Read Rev 1:1-3.

2. What do we learn about the source of Revelation, and what does this say to the seven churches and to Christians today?

3. What important theological lessons do we learn from the salutation to the seven churches in Asia? Who does John include in the salutation?

4. What do we learn from Rev 1:9 regarding the theology of Revelation? Remember that this passage outlines three important emphases for the theology and theme of Revelation.

5. What role does the vision of the triumphant Jesus play in Revelation and how does that vision affect Christians in the 21st century?

6. Discuss some of the striking emphases of Rev 1:17-20. How could these emphases encourage Christians and churches today?

A Closer Look

When we talk about the theology of a book or a passage, we refer to what may be learned about God and man from the text. In Revelation John emphases many attributes or characteristics of God. These things should not be reduced to sterile lists or statements, but should be seen as relevant to what is going on in John's situation and therefore to what is going on in our lives. The things we may know about God have significance for the human experience.

3

GOD'S IMPERFECT CHURCH

THE SEVEN LETTERS
REV 1:1-20

The Churches

The seven churches addressed by Jesus in Revelation 2 and 3 were not the only churches in Asia at the close of the first century A.D. We know of churches at Colossae and Heirapolis. However, seven in Jewish and early Christian numerology signified completeness. These letters, therefore, were addressed to all the churches in the region of Asia. The letters call the churches of Asia back to the centrality of their faith, namely faith in Jesus Christ. Churches have historically tended to supplant the core of their faith with matters of "churchness" or ecclesiological concerns such as church structure and church doctrine. This apparently was a problem faced by the churches in Asia. Church doctrine is important but only in so far as it informs Christian faith and points to Jesus, the foundation of that faith. Furthermore, churches have often compromised their faith by making concessions to their secular culture, often embracing materialism and tolerating sexual and moral perversion. In some cases, churches become comfortable in their religion, surrendering the alertness of a vigilant faith to the dangers or mediocrity. Each of these problems is encountered in five of the seven churches Revelation addresses (Ephesus, Sardis, Pergamum, Thyatira, and Laodicea) which were apparently prototypical of many of the churches in Asia at that time. Jesus sternly calls these churches to repentance and to the commitment of the former faith. Two churches (Smyrna and Philadelphia) are commended for their faithfulness and encouraged not to surrender the rewards of faithfulness under the pressures of cultural conformity.

> *Church doctrine is important but only in so far as it informs Christian faith and points to Jesus, the foundation of that faith.*

Jesus addresses each church by describing himself in terms drawn from John's vision of Jesus as the triumphant sovereign (Rev 1:12-16), thus personalizing the letters in a striking and powerful manner. In every instance Jesus assures the churches that he knows their labors and trials. This is both a sobering and encouraging thought! He knows everything about his church! Jesus addresses each letter to the angel of the church (angels are spiritual representatives, or guardian angels of the churches), thus drawing attention to the spiritual significance of each letter's message.

The seven letters, therefore, encourage the churches to examine their faith and commitment to Jesus in light of the impending challenges they will face at the hands of their pagan neighbors and the Roman Imperial Cult.

Conquering in Revelation!

In each of the seven letters (2:7,11, 17, 26; 3:5,12, 21) Jesus promises a reward to those who conquer (NIV overcome. We prefer the term conquer as it is in keeping with the military or combat terminology of Revelation). It will become apparent as Revelation unfolds that the conquerors are the martyrs, those who in refusing to compromise their faith in Jesus, die for that faith. Most of the rewards relate to either a promise of eternal life for dying, or the life sustaining spiritual food to be provided at the final banquet with God and Jesus.

Using grace as an excuse for sinful living should not be condoned by Christians of any age.

Ephesus – 2:1-7

Jesus, who is constantly walking around in the midst of his churches (2:1), commends Ephesus for being a hard working, faithful, doctrinally sound church. However, in spite of these fine attributes Jesus soundly rebukes the church for moving away from the love that once characterized this church. In the sharpest manner possible, Jesus calls the church to repentance. If they do not repent and return to love as their defining characteristic Jesus will come in judgment on them and remove their right tot be a church! The severity of Jesus' rebuke emphasizes how important it is for churches to understand that there is more to being a church than doctrinal exactitude and going through the motions of "doing church"! If Christian duty is not motivated by love for Jesus and for one another then it ceases to be acceptable to God. The Nicolaitans apparently were a sexually lascivious group of Christians who took grace to the extreme as an excuse for their worldliness. Jesus likewise condemned this attitude. Using grace as an excuse for sinful living should not be condoned by Christians of any age. For those who faithfully die as martyrs (conquer) Jesus promises the reward of eternal life.

Smyrna – 2:8-11

Smyrna was one of the two churches for which Jesus held no condemnation, only encouragement. Suffering slander and opposition, even persecution arising from the Jewish synagogue, Jesus recognized the faithfulness of this church and offered the reward of freedom from the second death (the final judgment, 20:14; 21:8).

Pergamum – 2:12-17

Pergamum was the capital of the Roman province of Asia with a magnificent citadel perched on a mountain one thousand feet above the valley below. The Roman Imperial cult flourished in Pergamum, boasting several impressive temples. The reference to Satan's throne was most likely in regard to the Roman governor's Imperial seat and the increasing persecution of Christians in that area. Balaam (Num 24 and 31; and 2 Peter 2:15) had become a symbol of compromise. There is always a tendency for Christians to compromise their commitment under opposition, especially the kind of persecution faced by Christians at the time of Revelation. Jesus warns against this. The hidden manna is a symbol drawn from Israel's wilderness wanderings under Moses, and is reference to the fact that God is able to sustain his people under the worst conditions, even persecution.

Thyatira – 2:18-29

Jesus commends the church at Thyatira for its works, love, and faith, and the fact that they have grown. Yet he admonishes them for tolerating a person, symbolized as Jezebel (1 Kings 16:29-30), who encourages immorality. The immorality is most likely associated with a pagan religious fertility rite. Jesus' condemnation of this tolerance is severe. Calling them to immediate repentance before he comes in judgment on them, he reminds the church that he searches both heart and mind, he knows their inner being. Jesus' promise of reward is important for the theology of Revelation. Those who conquer will reign with him on his throne (2:26-28). The concept of martyr-conquerors reigning with Jesus is an important thrust of the book.

Sardis – 3:1-6

The church at Sardis was guilty of an ailment that many churches suffer! They were spiritually asleep, especially to the dangers that faced them. They should have been alert and aware of the danger that threatened the church through compromise with local culture, but they were not, their works were not perfect or mature in God's sight. It seems that their religion was superficial. However, as in all churches, some are worthy. Worthiness in Revelation is associated with willingness to faithfully give witness to Jesus even if the price is one's life. The conqueror is promised a white robe, which in Revelation symbolizes victory and martyrdom.

Philadelphia – 3:7-13

Philadelphia is the other church in Revelation (the first was Smyrna) for which Jesus had no rebuke, only encouragement. This city was situated on a major crossroad and symbolized an open door to opportunity. Jesus promised them an open door to the riches of God's provision. The church in Philadelphia faced stern opposition from the Jewish synagogue. Jesus pronounced severe judgment on the synagogue when he judges those who persecute God's people. Jesus assured the church that this judgment was imminent (soon), and would have end of the world finality. Rather than God symbolically living in the synagogue, Jesus is promising the church that they will be the dwelling place of God.

Laodicea – 3:14-22

Worldly riches often plague Christians and churches. Too often Christians in an affluent culture reflect concern for secular recognition. The real danger is that

16

Christians often lean on their own ability to solve problems as they engage in the work of God. Such was the problem faced by the church at Laodicea. The result of relying on their own wealth was that they became lukewarm, loosing touch with the real power and dynamic of their religion, namely, faith and trust in God and his working. Jesus warns the church in Laodicea to be zealous and repent before it is too late for repentance. As always, Jesus stands outside the Christian's life and asks to be included. If Christians will allow Jesus entrance a rich blessing results, they will as conquerors reign with Jesus (3:21, sit with him on his throne).

The real danger is that Christians often lean on their own ability to solve problems as they engage in the work of God.

Summary of the Seven Letters

The letters to the seven churches remind us that God is fully aware of what goes on in the life of his church. He knows strengths and weaknesses. He calls all Christians to faithful witness without compromise with the secular world in which his people live. His reward to the conquerors (martyrs) for faithful witness is eternal life and reigning with Jesus in his kingdom.

These letters assure Christians in all ages that God cares for and sustains his church through every kind of trial. We all can become victorious conquerors over tribulation through our faith in Jesus.

❧ Reflection and Application

1. Becoming familiar with the names and locality of the seven churches in Asia will enhance your appreciation for their situation, and help clarify some of the reasons for John's urgent message. How are the seven churches related? What was going on in their lives?

2. List the central characteristics of each of the churches, both their strengths and weaknesses. What relationships do you see between these circumstances and those of churches today?

3. Select one of the letters and from it and plan a lesson that would be useful in your church. Are there songs that might fit well with the message of the letter you select?

4. In each of the letters there are themes that are repeated. What are they?

5. Who are the conquerors and what was their basic reward?

6. Spend time praying about the strengths and weaknesses you identified in question two. Ask God to help our churches realize that Jesus as the one who walks among the churches desires to be our guiding force as we face our spiritual battles.

4
IS GOD IN CONTROL?

THE SCROLL WITH SEVEN SEALS
REV 4:1-8:6

Introduction

This section opens with a heavenly scene with God on his throne. He is holding a scroll with seven seals which only Jesus can open. The opening of the seven seals progressively reveals that God does have a plan for the salvation of his creation and judgment of evil.

The Heavenly Scene – Rev: 4:1-11

This scene is of utmost importance to the theology of Revelation. The majestic picture of God on his throne reveals his absolute power over all creation. Around him are four living creatures and twenty-four elders who together sing praises to God's honor, power, and glory. The twenty-four elders in white robes represent martyrs through history who have sacrificed their lives to God. They and all creation worship God for his greatness. The four living creatures (Ezek 1:5ff, and Isa 6:1ff) proclaim and defend God's holiness.

John also sees what he describes as sea of glass before the throne. We will learn as we progress through Revelation that the sea in Hebrew tradition represents one of the mythological sources of evil. The sea of glass is before God's throne, but he controls it, – he controls evil! Later in 21:1 after God has judged Satan, the sea as a source of evil "is no more".

Evil fades in the presence of God's greatness and glory. No matter what creation has suffered at the hands of evil, no complaint comes from God's creation, for God is worthy to receive glory, honor, and power, for he created all things, and all things exist for his glory. It is imperative when facing suffering and trials that Christians understand the majesty of God's holiness, sovereignty, righteousness, and glory, and see the present in the light of this. God is able to transcend whatever may occur in the arena of history and human suffering.

The Scroll with Seven Seals – 5:1-14

The scroll John sees in God's hand is sealed with seven seals (seven symbolizes the scroll is completely sealed). No one is worthy to open the seals, which causes John great concern, for the scroll represents a plan that God has for the salvation of his creation and the judgment of evil. (Scrolls in the Hebrew tradition [Ezek 2:9, 10; Isa 29:11; Dan 12:4, et al.] signify that God has a plan for dealing with the crises his people are facing). Although no one seemingly is worthy to open the seals, Jesus as the Lamb is worthy, for he was martyred for his faith. By his martyrdom he has received a kingdom (reign) in which the saints have been made a kingdom of priests. Notice the connection of dying as a martyr, being worthy, and reigning in God's kingdom. Jesus as the Lamb was slain (martyred for his faith) and received a kingdom. Those ransomed by Jesus reign with him in this kingdom (5:9, 10). This is a major theme of Revelation: martyrs (conquerors) are promised that they will reign with Jesus (2:26-28; 3:21; 20:4-6). The scene continues with the twenty-four elders and four living creatures singing the glory of Jesus, the Lamb, who is worthy to receive all honor, power, and glory along with God.

The Seven Seals – 6:1-8:6

Here we witness the opening of six of the seven seals, but the scene is then interrupted by an interlude in Rev 7. The seventh seal follows the interlude and in turn introduces the next section of Revelation, the Seven Trumpets. The purpose of the interlude is to slow down the building crescendo of the six seals and reassure the saints that they need not fear God's judgments being announced in the seven seals.

The first four seals reveal four horsemen, the traditional "four horsemen of the apocalypse." Traditionally these horsemen have been understood to represent war, rebellion, famine, and death, all of which were a reminder to both the church and their opponents of the uncertainty of life, and the fact that God can use even the worst of conditions for his purpose.

The fifth seal is programmatic to the flow of thought developed by John in Revelation. It explains the fact that even martyrdom falls within the plan of God, and that God can and does use it for his purpose. Martyrdom as a sacrifice of faith to God is central to the theology of Revelation. God is worthy of such sacrifice. This scene reveals the martyrs beneath the sacrificial altar of God, crying out, asking when God plans to address their suffering. They are given white robes (martyrdom and victory robes) and encouraged to be patient until God's purpose has been fulfilled.

The sixth seal is fascinating in that it is the reader's first encounter with the unique language scholars identify as apocalyptic. It is an highly figurative, symbolic, and dramatic form of expression in which the suffering turn away from the here and now and cast their hope on God's divine intervention at some future time within his purpose. The apocalyptic mindset is extremely pessimistic about human potential and the flow of history, but highly optimistic that God will intervene in behalf of his servants.

The language we encounter in this passage, 6:12-15, is not new to those familiar with the Old Testament and the apocalyptic tradition of the Apocrypha. We encounter the symbolism of great earthquakes, the sun turning to darkness, the moon to blood, and the sky rolling up like a scroll in several places in the Old Testament, e.g., Isa 2:10-21; 13:10; 24:21-23; 34:2-4; Joel 2:28; Ezek 32:7. The same language is used in Matt 24:28ff. This language is designed to convey that God will bring judgment on those who oppress his people and who refuse to obey him. This sixth seal is intended to remind the Christians in Asia that God will, in his plan and in his time, bring fierce judgment on his enemies and the enemies of his people. The symbolism of God's ene-

20

mies trying to hide in caves (6:15, Isa 2:10ff.) and escape God's righteous judgments demonstrates the futility of such a plan. For these there is no escape from the wrath of God. The final clause is expressive, "who then can stand before the righteous wrath of God?" The interlude of chapter 7 is calculated to answer this question.

The Interlude – 7:1-17

It is important to see the connection between 7:1-17 and the question raised in 6:17, namely, "who can stand before it?" (the wrath of God). Revelation 7:1-8 explains that it is those who have been sealed with the seal of God who will escape the wrath of God. This "sealing" draws on passages such as Ex 12:3 where the seal of God on the door posts and lintels of the houses of the Israelites protected them when the angel of death passed over and killed the first born in Egypt. This "sealing" also recalls Ezek 9:1-11. Those with the seal of God do not need to fear his coming wrath on his enemies.

The creative listing of the twelve tribes of Israel stresses that this is not the literal twelve tribes of Israel that God has in mind. For instance, there is no mention of Dan, and Joseph rather than Ephraim is mentioned. Furthermore, Judah is listed first rather than Rueben, the eldest, who traditionally was mentioned first in a listing of the twelve tribes. However, Jesus was of the tribe of Judah! What is intended here is a reference to God's people through Jesus, symbolically referred to as the twelve tribes of Israel. Twelve thousand from each tribe is also symbolic; twelve representing God's people and one thousand signifying completeness (see Ps 50:10; 90:4; 91:7; 105:8; et al. where one thousand signifies completeness). All of God's people are sealed! We will learn from Rev 14:1 and other references that the numbering of God's people has a military or campaign symbolism. In chapter 7 the meaning John wishes to convey is that the people of God are on a military campaign and are thus protected by God. We might consider the one hundred and forty-four thousand to represent God's Church militant.

The next scene, 7:9-17, reveals a great multitude whom John learns represent all martyrs who have died in campaigns for God against evil. They came out of great tribulation, and are clothed in white robes washed in the blood of the lamb. No more will they hunger, thirst, or weep, for they are in the midst of the Lamb who wipes all tears from their eyes. They are victorious for "Salvation (victory) belongs to God and the Lamb" (7:10).

The interlude is intended to reassure the churches that they need not fear God's coming wrath, for they are sealed (protected) as God's church militant. Some, perhaps many, will die as martyrs in God's campaign against evil, but they need not fear either God's wrath or their death, for they and the Lamb are victorious.

The Seventh Seal – 8:1-6

The opening of the seventh seal is paradoxical in that it is significant enough for all of heaven to come to a standstill at its opening, but is anticlimactic in that it merely reveals seven warning trumpets of judgment that must be sounded against evil. An interesting and significant occurrence is the connection of the opening of the seventh

21

seal with the prayers at the golden alter. The opening of the seventh seal is an answer to the prayers of the saints in 6:10. The prayer was, "How long, God before you do something?" The answer of the seventh seal is, "Look, I am doing something. Be patient for a while longer and you will understand my purpose and plan!"

Seven angels now appear at the opening of the seventh seal with trumpets of warning judgments.

⁂ Reflection and Application

1. Carefully read Revelation 4. What does this throne room picture say about God? You may come up with several ways to describe the message of this text, think about and discuss the implications of this message for your life and the life of the church. How does this picture of God affect you when life is difficult? When life is easy? Does thinking about the picture presented in chapter 4 affect our worship?

2. What is the meaning of the scroll introduced in chapter 5? How do Ezek 2:9, 10; Isa 29:11; Dan 12:4 inform this?

3. What role does the prayer of the martyrs (6:10) play in the flow of argument John is presenting in the seven seals?

4. What role does the interlude of chapter 7 and the 144,000 play in Revelation?

5. Discuss from you own experience how God has been able to use trials and suffering in his purpose. Refer to the crucifixion and read Rom 5:3-5.

A Closer Look

The picture of God as sovereign and majestic makes a powerful statement in face of the threats the Asian churches experienced. Compare Ezek 1:5ff. and Isa 6:1ff., for similar scenes. What were the contexts for these passages? What was happening that made it important for Ezekiel and Isaiah to see those visions?

5

THE WARNING JUDGEMENTS

THE SEVEN TRUMPETS
REV 8:1-11:19

Introduction

Chapter 8 begins with the opening of the seventh seal which initiates thirty minutes of silence in heaven. This silence symbolizes the intense expectation of the revelation of the seventh seal. The seventh seal revealed seven trumpets. The seven trumpets call evil men to repentance (9:20) before God's severe judgment comes upon them.

These judgments, like the sixth seal, demand another interlude to break the increasing tension involved in the process of the trumpets being blown. This interlude comes in chapters 10 and 11. We encounter the seventh (final) trumpet in 11:15-19.

The Seven Trumpets – 8:1-11:19

The first four trumpets draw their images from the plagues of Egypt. Their purpose is the same, to cause evil men to think and to repent before the mighty power of God. Figures like great earthquakes would be familiar to those living in Asia where such were common. A burning mountain falling into the sea was familiar in Jewish tradition, symbolizing the judgment of ancient Babylon and a kingdom coming under the judgment of God. The image of a great star falling from heaven into the waters would likewise be understood as a judgment of God on an earthly power. John draws on imagery from Isaiah 14:12-15 where God's judgment on the king of Babylon is described as a star falling from heaven. In Revelation the star represents Rome, Satan's evil agent, being judged with the same severity with which God judged ancient Babylon.

The fourth trumpet announces a judgment in apocalyptic language similar to the sixth seal, a third of the sun and the moon are struck and a third of the stars are kept from shining. The symbolism of one third implies that these judgments were not final, but intended to cause evil men to repent. At the conclusion of the fourth trumpet an eagle announces three woes to be sounded by the next three trumpets. The eagle (or vulture) flying in the mid-heaven was considered a bird of carrion and a harbinger of doom and death.

The fifth trumpet reveals again a star falling from heaven. As already noted, the star represents the evil king of Babylon. This star was given the key to the bottomless pit (a source of evil in Hebrew mythology), and from this abyss a frightening swarm of locusts emerge. The background of this locust image is the prophetic book of Joel and God's judgment on Judah and Jerusalem. In Revelation the locusts represent a fierce and evil army released to bring suffering on humanity. But, they are controlled and limited in their destruction. They are not permitted to bring their judgment on those sealed with the seal of God (Rev 7, the 144,000). The leader of this evil army is called destruction (Abaddon and Apollyon, Hebrew and Greek terms meaning destruction and ruin).

The sixth trumpet reveals an awesome and sinister army from across the Euphrates (depicting the Persians who were a constant threat to Rome). This fearsome army, like the locusts, brings a partial judgment on the earth. The purpose of these partial judgments is to call evil men to repentance before the seventh and final trumpet is sounded. Despite the severity of these plagues or trumpets, mankind did not repent of their evil and idolatry (9:20).

The next vision should be the seventh trumpet which would bring this series of judgments to finality. However, again we encounter an interlude that interrupts the flow of the visionary judgments. The interlude includes a little scroll, a measuring rod, and two witnesses who are slain.

The "Little" Scroll – 10:1-11

John sees a mighty angel dressed in divine regalia standing with a "little" scroll open in his hand. The divine regalia implies that this angel and his message come from the divine presence. The fact that he is a mighty angel suggests that his message is significant. That the little book is open implies that the message is immediate. Most likely the fact that it is referred to as a "little" scroll infers that its message is related to the message of the larger scroll, of which it certainly is a sub-section. John is told not even to write the message of the angel down, for its message (unlike Daniel's of Dan 12) is immediate, and that there should be no more delay. That there should be no more delay ties this message back to the prayers of the martyrs in Rev 6:10 and the angel of 8:3 who offered the prayers of the saints on the golden altar. They had cried "How long...," now the answer comes, "No more delay...." We should remember also that we are in the visions of the seven trumpets of judgment and anticipating the seventh and last such trumpet.

They had cried "How long...," now the answer comes, "No more delay..."

John is instructed to eat the little scroll. Its message would be bitter to the stomach but sweet to the mouth. The meaning is drawn from Ezek 3:3. The angel's bitter message was that martyrdom was inevitable. However, the sweet message to the martyrs was that God promised them a triumphant victory – resurrection.

Finally, John is informed that he must again repeat the message of his revelation. Most infer from this that Revelation 1-11 forms the first act of the revelatory drama, and Revelation 12-22 the second act which repeats in more specific symbolism the message of the act one.

The Measuring of the Temple – 11:1-3

This paragraph is one of several enigmatic passages in Revelation. The measuring of the temple and city draws from Ezek 40, the forty-two months and one thousand two hundred and sixty days from Dan 7 and 12 (3 1/2 years = 42 months = 1260 days). This paragraph assures the saints that God knows them, has sealed them, and will protect them even though they are persecuted. They will be persecuted (42 months in Daniel represents a period of trial and persecution) and will have to die for their faith, but God will not desert them, for he has sealed them and assured them as conquerors of victory through the resurrection. The message of dying and being resurrected, being conquered yet conquering, is heightened in the next vision of two olive trees and lampstands.

The Two Olive Trees and Lampstands – 11:4-14

In this paragraph John is at his creative best! He draws on a number of well known Old Testament symbols and as a consummate impressionistic artist paints a dynamic picture of the church witnessing, being persecuted, dying as martyrs in "disgrace", but being raised triumphantly by the power of God to positions of glory.

The two olive trees and lampstands are drawn from Zech 4 and represent faithful witnesses to God. Like Elijah (who had power to close the skies to rain) and Moses (who brought the plagues on Egypt) these "prophets" witness faithfully against stern opposition. Unlike Elijah and Moses, however, they are killed for their efforts. They lie in the streets of the wicked city which is likened to Sodom, Egypt and Jerusalem, all of which persecuted God's people. For this, these cities were all severely judged by God (remember, Jerusalem has by now been destroyed by Rome, God's agents, just as Jesus had promised). But as in the vision of Ezek 37, the dry bones of God's people are brought back to life, vindicated in the presence of their enemies, and taken up victoriously to be with God. One can hardly escape seeing parallels to Jesus' suffering servanthood, death, and vindication to glory and reign in Philippians 2.

This scene closes with John's reminder that two of the three woes have passed and that only the third remains!

The Seventh Trumpet – 11:15-19

The seventh warning trumpet or judgment announces that God has taken up his reign and through Jesus has pronounced his judgment on evil. The twenty-four elders, representatives of all martyrs, give thanks to God that he has exercised his great power and shown his sovereign reign. From the very presence of God's ark of the covenant come flashes of lightening and peals of thunder, authenticating his divine action.

We should remember that Rev 1-11 is merely the first act of this great drama and that the judgments we have been witnessing are warning judgments calling on the oppressors of God's people to repent. They do not heed the warning! We are now ready for Act II in which the same message will be revealed but with greater clarity and specificity, and specific finality.

🎵 Reflection and Application

1. What role do the seven trumpets play in Revelation and how are they related to the seven seals?

2. What was the significance of the silence in heaven for thirty minutes (8:1)?

3. We have stated that the purpose of the judgments of the seven trumpets is to call people to repentance. What does this teach us about God? Think of Old Testament stories of judgement. What is God's purpose in judgement?

4. What is the meaning of the "little" scroll and John eating it? What is the Old Testament background behind this?

5. The message of the little scroll is a promise of resurrection for those who died for the faith. American Christians are unfamiliar with the threat of dying for the faith. Does this relative comfort threaten our discipleship?

6. What message can we learn from Revelation 11, the measuring of the temple and the two olive branches?

7. What contemporary messages can we learn from the seven trumpets?

A Closer Look

The events of these seven trumpets remind us that although evil is inevitable, given the work of Satan, God will judge evil. However, before he judges evil he gives people the opportunity to repent. Furthermore, God can and does use evil men and nations to bring about his purpose. We see an example of this in God's judgment and destruction of Jerusalem. He used an evil nation, Rome, to bring abut his judgment on Jerusalem.

6

THE LAMB - GOD'S ANSWER TO EVIL

SIGNS OF DISTRESS AND DELIVERANCE
REV 12:1-14:5

Introduction

The theological answer to the problem of evil in Revelation reaches its high point in this section. The focus is on Jesus, the king of God's kingdom, and as such, "the ruler of kings on earth" (1:5). In this section we encounter seven unnumbered figures, 1) the woman with child, 2) the dragon, 3) the male child, 4) the archangel Michael, 5) the beast from the sea, 6) the beast from the earth, 7) the Lamb on mount Zion.

The First Three Figures - "The Messianic Community" - 12:1-6

As we follow the unfolding of the first three of these seven figures it is almost impossible to miss the parallels to the Christ birth narrative. There is the messianic community (the woman) awaiting the birth of the child; the dragon or Satan (Herod), attempting to thwart the birth; and finally the male child Messiah and the persecuted messianic community (the church) after the ascension of the Messiah. The message these figures convey to the church is that Satan has historically attempted to impede God's plan. Even before the birth of Jesus the faithful messianic community had experienced pagan and Roman opposition. Satan did all he could to prevent the ministry of Jesus from developing (Herod's treachery and Jesus' temptation). Even in the death of Jesus, Satan was behind the scene (the Jews, Judas, and the Pilate were merely the agents of Satan). But God triumphed, raising Jesus from the dead. The church needed to understand that Satan would continue his deceit and opposition to God, expending all of his energy now on the church. The church will, however, with God's help triumph over Satan. Furthermore, Michael (who never loses a battle) is on their side!

> *The message of the cosmic drama is that Satan has already been defeated, God and Christ are already victorious, and Jesus is already reigning in God's eternal Kingdom.*

The Fourth Figure - Michael and the War in Heaven - 12:7-17

In Hebrew tradition Michael is the undefeated prince of God's heavenly army. The message for the church is that it should decide whose side to be on, Satan's or Michael's! It is tempting for the reader to try to fix a date in history for this heavenly battle. But apocalyptic literature is concerned not with the when of an "event", but rather what "the event" intends to say. The message of the cosmic drama is that Satan has already been defeated, God and Christ are already victorious, and Jesus is already reigning in God's eternal Kingdom. Quests to determine when these cosmic events will occur tend to miss the point of the message.

Through Christ's victory over Satan, the martyrs become conquerors with Jesus. They have participated in God's victory through the blood of the Lamb (Jesus' martyrdom on the cross) and the word (message) of their testimony (their own martyrdom), "for they loved not their lives even unto death" (12:10,11).

But the dragon (Satan) is still a threat to God's creation. He turns the nations against God's people (the woman or messianic community) and pursues and persecutes them. However, as we have already learned from the first act of this drama, the people of God are sealed and protected (7:3).

The Fifth Figure – The Sea Beast – 13:1-10

The next thing John sees is a beast rising out of the sea. Remember, the sea in Hebrew mythology is one of the sources of evil. The concept of a sea beast as an evil entity was not new for Hebrew mythology and literature. The Old Testament speaks of such a sea beast, Leviathan (Job 3:8, 41:1; Ps 74:14; 105:26; and Isa 27:1). In fact Hebrew literature speaks also of an earth beast, Behemoth, whom we will shortly encounter in the next paragraph of this mythological drama! (See 2 Esdras 6:49-52 in the Apocrypha[1] for this reference.) Since many will not have 2 Esdras readily available, and since this is an significant text for Revelation, we include it here for reference:

> [49] "Then thou didst keep in existence two living creatures; the name of one thou didst call Behemoth and the name of the other Leviathan. [50] And thou didst separate one from the other, for the seventh part where the water had been gathered together could not hold them both. [51] And thou didst give Behemoth one of the parts which had been dried up on the third day, to live in it, where there are a thousand mountains; [52] but to Leviathan thou didst give the seventh part, the watery part; and thou hast kept them to be eaten by whom thou wilt, and when thou wilt."

From John's use of Daniel and other sources in Revelation we understand this sea beast to represent a political power, namely, the *civil power* of Imperial Rome. The reference to one of the heads of this beast receiving a mortal wound which was healed is most likely a reference to the *Nero Redivivus* myth that Nero would return in some form and continue his evil persecution of God's people. The Roman Emperors by claiming to be divine rulers thus blasphemed God. The beast is allowed to persecute God's people and to conquer them, but we already know from previous references in Revelation, conquered saints become the real conquerors! It is important for understanding the background of this text that one read Daniel 7 at this point, and

---

[1] See A Closer Look in this chapter.

especially Dan 7:13, 14, 22, 25-27. John's use of Daniel should not be interpreted as a fulfillment of Daniel. John uses Daniel typologically.[2]

> "Those who dwell on earth" are deceived by the blasphemy of the beast and in turn worship it. As we progress through Revelation John will further define "those who dwell on the earth" as those who follow the beast, persecute the saints, and receive the mark of the beast.

The proverbial saying of Rev 13:10 identifies the persecution of saints as inevitable in view of the sociological and political climate in Asia at the time. The saints are therefore called to faithful endurance under this persecution. Life will always be full of trials and suffering, this is inevitable in a world under the power of sin. (Rom 3:10). Christians are called to witness to their faith and trust in God's power in Christ to transform even the worst suffering into victory.

The Sixth Figure – Earth Beast – Rev 13:11-18

Although Behemoth is mentioned by name only once in the Old Testament (Job 4:15) and not at all in the New Testament, his role in Hebrew mythology was well attested as above in 2 Esdras 6:49-52. As Leviathan was symbolic of an evil power from the sea, so too was Behemoth a symbol of evil power, but this time from the earth. John draws on this two-fold myth to demonstrate the two-fold evil power of Rome. Leviathan represented the civil power of Rome. Behemoth symbolizes the religious power of the Roman imperial cult of emperor worship. We learn from history and archaeology that almost every major city of the Roman world housed either one of more temples to the Roman deities and Emperors. Pergamum was a striking example of this. Behemoth, who looks like a lamb but speaks like a dragon, epitomizes this quasi-religious power which seduces people into worship the emperor as a divine being. Those who refuse to worship the image of the emperor are slain (martyred). Those who worship the emperor receive the mark of the beast on either their right hand or forehead. Identifying the beast from the mark or number of the beast (666) has challenged commentators on Revelation throughout the centuries, without anything like a consensus ever being reached. It is doubtful that John had any one specific emperor in mind! He does not, however, leave us in limbo over this interesting conundrum, for he tells us clearly that this beast is not a divine being, but a human being because his number "is a human number" (NIV "it is a man's number"). It is clear that this second quasi-religious beast, Behemoth, (symbolizing the

Life will always be full of trials and suffering, this is inevitable in a world under the power of sin.

---

[2] Typology is a literary term that describes one event, person, or thing that foreshadows or bears some resemblance to another.

Imperial cult) drew on the power and authority of the first beast, Leviathan (representing the civil power of Rome) leading men to worship the emperor as a divine being. Christians refused to do this. This inevitably lead to their persecution and martyrdom. Thankfully, John does not leave us at this point faced by these two evil beasts, for the next vision is of The Lamb on Mount Zion, from where God symbolically rules his people.

The Seventh Figure - Lamb on Mount Zion – 14:1-5

The contrast between the previous two beasts and the lamb is striking! It is the lamb who stands on Mount Zion ruling over God's creation, not the earth beast, Rome! With him are the 144,000, each with the name of the lamb and God's name written on their foreheads! They belong to the Lamb and to God, not to the beast! The symbolism of the 144,000 being chaste draws on Hebrew combat ritual in which God's army have consecrated themselves to God and to the battle. Nothing comes between them and their purpose. (Read Deut 20; 23:9,10; and 1 Sam 21:4,5.) The 144,000 symbolize the church militant, consecrated, and victorious. The 144,000 have not worshipped the beast, for "in their mouth no lie was found, for they are spotless."

Summary of the Seven Unnumbered Figures

The message intended by these seven figures is clear. Satan, who tried to defeat God's purpose at the birth of the Messiah, will continue his evil purpose by attacking the church through the Roman Imperial cult . This would cause many to worship the beast and receive its number or sign of ownership. In contrast to this those who refuse to compromise their faith in Jesus, the Lamb, by worshipping the beast received his and the Father's name as a sign of ownership. As God's consecrated church militant they suffer martyrdom but are not be defeated. The conquered become the conquerors! They stand with the Lamb on Mount Zion, and with the Lamb they reign over God's creation.

⁂ Reflection and Application

1. What is the overall message of the seven unnumbered visions of Rev 13, 14?

2. How would this relate to Christians living in the 21st century?

3. What does the sea beast, Leviathan, symbolize, and how does the land beast, Behemoth, relate to this?

4. What does the number 666 symbolize in Rev 13:18? How do we know this? What does this mean for the church in the 1st century, and for the church today?

5. What does it mean that the saints stand on Mount Zion with the Lamb?

A Closer Look

The Aprocrypha serves as a helpful resource in understanding Revelation and its symbolism, for this collection of writings falls basically between the Old and New Testament periods. It covers periods of Jewish persecution and employs much the same symbolic language as Revelation. The Apocryphal writings, although treasured by Judaism, were never considered by the Judeo-Christian tradition to be on the same level as the canonical writings. In the Catholic tradition they are included along with the canonical writings of the Old and New Testaments.

The book of Daniel, which likewise speaks to God's people in suffering persecution, also serves as a helpful resource of ideas and images for John in Revelation. The connection between Daniel and Revelation is not one of prophecy and fulfillment, but one of images that typologically enrich John's visions in Revelation.

7

INTERLUDE

MESSAGES OF GOD'S MERCY
REV 14:6-20

Introduction

In typical style we encounter another interlude! Before the vision of God's consummated judgments are described, which symbolize the finality and completeness of his judgment of Rome and Satan, John again stresses the holiness, righteousness and sovereignty of God. In these seven unnumbered messages God again calls evil to repentance. In John's drama, the martyrs have cried out "How long before you avenge us of our blood" (6:10). "Why does God not bring his decisive judgment on this evil world?" "What is holding God's judgment back?" For hurting Christians it seems that God has given an over abundance of time to an evil world. In Revelation John assures the saints that God will judge the evil world in his time. In similar fashion, 2 Peter 3:8-10 addresses concerns over why God permits an evil world to continue to exist. Peter reminds Christians suffering persecution that God is not slow concerning judgment. In his holiness, righteousness, and sovereignty, God determines to give all people ample time and opportunity for repentance. This lesson of understanding the tension between the justice of God and his holiness, righteousness, and sovereignty has never been easy for humans to understand. The Old Testament prophet Jonah and Israel had difficulty understanding how God could be patient with, and forgive an evil Gentile world.

In his holiness, righteousness, and sovereignty, God determines to give all people ample time and opportunity for repentance.

Under stress, Christians also often loose sight of the extraordinary loving kindness of God. In the Hebrew Old Testament there is a concept (hesed) which is translated in the RSV as "steadfast love." Hesed or "the steadfast love of the Lord" becomes a dominant concept in understanding the nature of God in the Old Testament. It appears over 150 times in Psalms written by believers under great stress. Hesed reminds believers that in spite of their suffering God is still there in his steadfast loving kindness to recompense them in the end. Hesed's best known reference is in Lamentations 3:21-27 where lamenting over the awful tragedy that had befallen Israel,

Jeremiah is reminded of God's "steadfast love which endures forever, whose mercy never comes to an end." Because Lamentations 3:21-27 is so relevant to the discussion in Revelation, please read this passage.

In the seven angelic messages of Revelation 14 we encounter this same loving kindness and patience of God, this time hesed is available to the evil world of the two beasts. Cries for vengeance and vindication (6:10) must be moderated and balanced by an understanding of God's holy, righteous, and sovereign purpose, even his "steadfast love" for this rebellious and evil world.

The Seven Angelic Messages

John numbers only the first three angelic messages, leaving the following four to the reader to identify. The first angel brings an eternal gospel message to "those who dwell on the earth" (the persecutors of God's people). It is an eternal gospel indicating the eternal nature of God's redemptive purpose. The gospel message calls for those who are oppressing God's people to repent and worship God, not the emperor. It is God alone who is deserving of worship and glory! No human being who bears a human number (666), no matter how powerful, is worthy of worship! There is a essence of urgency in this gospel call (as in the whole message of Revelation) for the hour of God's judgment has come and is certain; God will not restrain his judgment for long. This message is also a strident reminder to the saints to resist any temptation to worship the emperor.

The second angelic message builds on the first. Recalling the judgment of Babylon, John cites both Isaiah 21:9 and Jeremiah 51:8,9. It will be helpful for the student to read these two significant passages. One should remember that when these statements were made in Isaiah and Jeremiah Babylon was still standing! However, Babylon's judgment was certain, for God in his eternal purpose had already judged Babylon with end of the world judgment and finality! In this text, for the first time in Revelation, we encounter a symbolic reference to Babylon. In the New Testament Babylon is encountered 12 times in 11 verses. Four of those references were to Babylon of old. In the remaining seven texts (six of them in Revelation, one in 1 Pet 5:13) the symbolic reference is to Rome. The literature of the first three centuries is precise in this association. Rome, because of its evil nature and eventual doom, is likened to Babylon. God has already judged Rome with the same judgment he brought on Babylon of old. The warning to the Christians and to those who bore the mark of the beast was clear; worship only God! Worship the emperor and Rome and you will experience God's decisive end of the world judgment, the same as he poured out on Babylon of old.

The third angelic message likewise flows out of the previous two messages. Worship the beast and you will receive its mark and consequently "drink" (experience) God's wrath poured out undiluted in his judgment of Rome. Revelation 14:12 adds decisively to this warning, "this is a call for the endurance of the saints...."

The following four angelic messages are not numbered as the first three, but it is possible to identify their message, or action. The fourth angelic message pronounces a blessing on those who die faithfully in the Lord, that is, those who have refused to worship the beast and who have died as martyrs. They will be given rest from their labors or suffering. Although this is a promise specifically given to reassure the martyrs, its message or blessing is firm for all who die faithfully in the Lord.

The fifth angelic message was one unequivocally related to judgment. The initial reference is to Daniel 7, but the applied inference is to the Son of Man, Jesus, who is to judge the world in righteousness (Acts 17:30, 31). This angel comes right from the temple (presence) of God, implying that the message originates from God himself. The message is to bring judgment on Rome, for the time has come for Rome to be judged with end of the world judgment or significance.

The sixth angel arrives on the scene with a sickle to assist in the judgment. Another angel, presumably the seventh and final angel, appears and gives instruction for the judgment to begin. This angel comes from the altar in the temple, connecting God's judgment with the prayers of the saints from beneath the altar (6:10). God is answering the martyr's prayers for vindication! The severity of God's judgment on Rome is dramatized by the symbolic extent to which blood flows from the harvest; a flow of blood approximately four feet deep and two hundred miles long!

Summary of the Angelic Messages and Actions

Whenever Christians experience trials and persecution there is the tendency to look for immediate response and vindication. Revelation, and especially this section of seven angelic messages, encourages Christians to be patient while God works his eternal purpose. Christians need to be assured that God has heard their cry and will respond. His seeming delay is not accidental; out of his hesed (steadfast love) God is concerned that all persons, even the evil, have an opportunity to repent. Ultimately, in his eternal purpose he has already judged the persecutors with end-of-the-world judgment. The martyrs are encouraged to endure while God works his eternal purpose.

✷ Reflection and Application

1. How does this interlude relate to the Parable of Wheat and Tares in Matt 13:24-30, and 36-43?

2. How does this section relate to Jesus' teaching on Matt 7:1-5 and Paul in Rom 14:13-16?

3. Often Christians are judged or criticized by other persons, sometimes unjustly and harshly. How would these angelic messages relate to such Christian contexts today?

4. What encouragement can we draw from these angelic messages? Relate the message of hesed to contemporary crises and situations.

A Closer Look

Read the book of Jonah. We all recall Jonah's disobedience to God concerning his commission to preach to the Assyrians, but it is easier to understand his resistance when we consider the wickedness of his intended audience. Do some research on the Assyrians and note the parallels to the evil Roman Empire of John's day. What does all of this say about God?

8

GOD'S CONSUMMATED JUDGEMENTS

SEVEN BOWLS OF WRATH
REV 15:1-16:21

Introduction

Revelation 15 is in many ways styled after chapter 4. We are transported back to God's heavenly throne room, the four living creatures, and the twenty-four elders singing the praises of the Lord God Almighty. The glass-like sea is mingled with the purifying fire of God. Beside the sea (not threatened by it) are the martyrs who have conquered the beast and its image. We also see seven angels with seven plagues, which represent seven bowls of God's wrath. These plagues of God's wrath are the last, for with them we encounter God's final judgment on the two beasts (Rome, in its civil and Imperial cult power) and those who dwell on the earth (those who worship the beast and who persecute God's people). With these plagues the wrath of God on Rome is brought to finality ("is ended").

The Seven Bowls of God's Wrath - 16:1-21

The implications of these bowls of God's wrath are so serious and significant that the temple in heaven itself comes to a complete standstill; no one can enter it until the bowls are poured out. The instruction to pour out the seven bowls of God's wrath comes from within the temple, implying that the instructions come from God himself. We learn an interesting phenomenon about apocalyptic judgments from this text. Although men are being judged, apocalyptic judgments are often expressed against the physical creation. The reason is that the apocalyptist sees the whole creation involved in humanity's sin. Here we see the seven bowls of God's wrath symbolically poured out on the earth (16:1). Romans 8:18-25 is an interesting expression of the same form of symbolism. In the context of suffering Paul speaks of the whole creation suffering and longing for the revelation of the sons of God. The hope of the whole creation lies in God's redemptive activity.

The first four bowls of wrath are reminiscent of the Egyptian plagues. They are poured out on the physical creation. The first is poured out on the earth and evil sores break out on those who dwell on the earth (those who worship the beast and persecute God's people). The second bowl is poured out on the sea which becomes like the blood of dead men. The third bowl turns the rivers of water into blood. Nevertheless, the angel of the water recognizes that this is a just judgment in response to the persecution of the saints. The martyrs beneath the altar of God (6:10) agree!

John's intention is that we recognize God's judgments, however harsh, as righteous judgments, and that we see the connection between these bowls of wrath and the prayers for vindication from the martyrs (6:10). The fourth bowl is poured out on the sun demonstrating the power of God's judgments. Unfortunately, those who dwell on the earth do not repent and give God the glory!

The next three bowls of wrath are more demonic. They are expressed more directly against the throne of the beast, namely, Rome. The fifth bowl turns the kingdom into darkness and men are torn with anguish. We are reminded that Rome, although powerful, was never above internal intrigue, inner suspicion, and terrorism. Men now curse the God of these plagues, but they still refuse to repent!

The sixth bowl brings us to the fascinating battle of Armageddon. So much misleading information has been disseminated concerning this figure of speech that it is difficult to break away from some of these impressions. However, if we remember to set these figures in the context of what is being discussed, a solution is not always that difficult. We are reminded that the context of the message of Revelation is about things (crises) that would soon break into the experience of the 1st century church in Asia (1:1, 3). The crises related to the persecution of the church at the hands of the Jews, pagan culture, and Roman governors in Asia. The church was facing severe persecution and Christians were already dying as martyrs for their faith. The martyrs had cried out to God for vindication. The seven bowls of wrath are in response to those prayers. Those who dwell on the earth, and the throne of the beast (Rome) are being judged by God. The symbolic "battle of Armageddon" we encounter here is set in this context. The battle we are seeing so dramatically described in this text represents the battle between God and Satan being played out between the saints and Rome in Asia. This battle has no reference to the end of the world other than that it is described in end of the world language for dramatic effect. This is not as predicted by premillennial theories, the end of the world, or some war between the Arabs and Israel that will usher in Jesus' final victory over evil and his one thousand year reign in Jerusalem .

This sixth bowl presents a figurative battle in which the waters of the great Euphrates river are dried up to prepare the way for the kings of the east. The imagery is reminiscent of how ancient Babylon was defeated by the Medo-Persians in 539 B.C. Herodotus records that the Medes captured the city by damning the river Euphrates and entering the city under the gates protecting access to the city by river. Impregnable Babylon fell when no one expected it. This was in keeping with Jeremiah's prediction that the Medes would be the agents of God in the fall of ancient Babylon. Figuratively, Rome (the new Babylon) will fall as did Babylon of old. The symbolism of the three frogs speaks of the demonic power exercised by the beast and false prophet (the civil and religious cults of Rome). Symbolically Rome and the kings of the world that had been seduced by Rome's power would be gathered for this battle, but they would loose, for God and Michael (12:7) never loose a battle, especially when it is fought at the Mount of Megiddo!

But what are the roots of this fascinating reference to Armageddon? Among much speculation and discussion the most reasonable conclusion is that the term Armageddon is derived from the Hebrew *har*, meaning hill or mountain, and Megiddo an ancient city fortress at the western end of the plain of Esdraelon and Jezreel. The fortress at Megiddo has an ancient history dating back well beyond Israel's occupation. Under King Solomon the "mountain" fortress became a stronghold for Israel and protection against attacks from the North and East. Megiddo was the scene of great battles between Israel and her foes, and one symbolizing fortitude and victory. John uses the term *har-Megiddo* symbolically in reference to the great battle to be waged between God and the beast, a battle which God will win as he always does when Michael leads his hosts into battle. In modern parlance we might symbolically refer to someone meeting his Waterloo. Armageddon, therefore, symbolizes the battle between God and Rome, not the end of the world battle–an interpretation which lifts the battle out of the context of chapter 16 and Revelation as a whole.

The seventh angel poured his bowl into the air and in a loud voice cried "It is done!" God's judgment on the beast, the new Babylon, has been accomplished. The loud voice is accompanied by earthquakes and other apocalyptic symbols implying that God's judgment had been fully poured out on Rome, the beast. We recall the statement in 15:1 that with these, the last plagues, the wrath of God was ended or completed.

It is imperative when following the visions of Revelation that one does not perceive the visions or scenes to be sequential. Most often they are repetitive, dramatizing the same event repeatedly for vivid impact. Some commentators have called this phenomenon "recapitulation." Perhaps a better way of expressing this is that we encounter "a rebirth of images." In the next section, (17:1-20:15) the same judgments of God against the new Babylon, Rome, will be repeated demonstrating dramatically God's absolute authority over evil and the beast, Rome.

Summary of the Seven Bowls of Wrath

John clearly informs his readers that these plagues about to be poured out of the seven bowls of God's wrath are the last. They represent God's final and complete judgment of the beast, Babylon/Rome. With them God's wrath against Rome is perfected or consummated! The beast will mount a fierce battle to be fought at a battleground symbolically named *har-Megiddo*. This battle will be decisive. God wins! This battle is not the final end of the world battle, but merely a symbolic battle demonstrating God's power and victory over Rome.

᪾ Reflection and Application

1. Why does John repeat the images of Rev 4 in chapter 15? What is the gist of this point, and what contemporary application might it have for Christians today? Pay attention to the song of the martyr saints.

2. What is the implication of the angel's proclamation in 16:5-7, "just and holy are thy judgments"? What might we learn from this?

3. Describe some *har-Megiddo* type battles Christians might be called on to fight in their personal lives today? What are the implications of such battles?

4. How can it help Christians to know that God has judged the beast (Rome) with final judgment while the beast still causes great harm? What lesson is there in this for Christians today? Be specific in your applications.

9

God's Triumph Over Evil

Rome Will Not Stand
Rev 17:1-20:15
Part One

Introduction

In this section we see the judgments of God on Babylon described in greater detail and specificity than in the previous section. We are reminded that the visions, or series of visions in Revelation are not normally sequential. In the terms used by many commentators they recapitulate or repeat previous visions. We prefer to call this process a rebirth of images in which previous images are given new life or definition. In providing more specific definition to the judgments poured out in the seven bowls of God's wrath we will notice that Babylon, not simply the beast and the false prophet are the objects of God's judgments. Furthermore, it becomes obvious that John is in reality focusing attention on the character of Rome by his references to the enemy as Babylon the Great.

Although John does not specifically number the seven descriptions of God's authority it is possible to identify in this section seven examples of God's sovereign rule. The seven unnumbered descriptions of God's authority appear to be: 1) The character of Babylon is described, 2) The doom of Babylon is announced, 3) The marriage supper of the Lamb is pictured, 4) The defeat of the beast and false prophet is guaranteed, 5) The binding of Satan is assured, 6) The reign of the martyrs is vouched for, and 7) The final judgment is introduced. In this lesson we will discuss the first three of these descriptions. The final four will be discussed in the next lesson.

The Character of Babylon is Described - 17:1-18

The true character of Babylon is revealed to John by one of the seven angels pouring out the bowls of God's wrath in the previous section. This almost unnoticed technique is John's way of connecting the seven descriptions of God's divine authority to the judgments described in the seven bowls of God's wrath. This demonstrates that the seven descriptions in this section are not the consequence of the previous judgments, but a recapitulation of the seven bowls in greater specificity.

The first point John makes is that Babylon is to be compared with a harlot whose seductive power beguiles the nations who become intoxicated by her powerful allure.

That John has Rome in mind becomes clearer as his description of this seductive woman develops. In the final verse of Rev 17 he declares that "the woman is the great city which has dominion over the kings of the earth." It is obvious that the only city with this power in John's day and in the life of the church of the 1st century was Rome. In 17:6 John describes this woman as being "drunk with the blood of the saints and the blood of the martyrs of Jesus Christ." This is the first and only occurrence of the word *martyr* in the KJV, the ASV, and the RSV. The NIV and the NASV translate this as *witnesses*. The point we wish to make is that witnessing in Revelation is a synonym for martyrdom. The harlot, or great city being described in this section is responsible for the blood of the saints shed in martyrdom. Again, this focuses attention on Rome as the harlot Babylon. John is not attempting to conceal this identification or to write in a secret code. He is simply drawing attention to the real sinister character of Rome. She is like Babylon of old, evil to the core. She is to be compared to a harlot who seduces her clients. She is responsible for the blood of the saints and will be held accountable for this as was Babylon of old. Seated on a scarlet beast which speaks blasphemous words and has seven heads and ten horns connects this woman to the beast of Rev 13, and again clarifies the fact that this woman is associated with the political or civil power of Rome.

The next block of material which speaks of seven kings, and an eighth that follows, has provided commentators with endless opportunities for speculation! Attempts to identify these kings with specific emperors, while appearing to be historically impressive, is not well supported by history itself. Neither does it fit into the scheme of what John is describing. That he symbolically refers to seven kings in Revelation is not surprising! The point he is making draws on what we have previously described as a Nero Redivivus myth, in which Romans and Christians feared that Nero would reappear again and resume his atrocities. Most likely the beast that was, is not, and is to ascend from the bottomless pit is a reference to Nero and the fear that he would reappear. The point is that this king comes from the bottomless pit (i.e., he is evil) and will go on to perdition (ruin). The eighth king incorporates all of the evil of the previous seven, including Nero, and continues the evil work of the seven. However, he, too, goes on to perdition! No matter how powerful the eight kings are, they are evil. But they all will be judged by God and go on to perdition (ruin).

The ten horns or ten kings who receive limited authority from the beast are the client kings who were either conquered by Rome and permitted to govern for Rome, or kings who were seduced by the power and glory of Rome and surrendered to the sovereignty of Rome. The fascinating statement that the ten kings and the beast who are seduced by the harlot turn against her is a reference to the constant turmoil and insecurity that existed in Rome. God uses this insecurity to his purpose.

Finally, the climax to the whole discussion is that the harlot, the eight kings, and the ten client kings make war on the lamb and are defeated. This is the theme that we have seen repeated on several occasions in Revelation. The devil fights against Michael and is defeated. The dragon and the beast assemble the kings of the world for a great battle at har-Megiddo, and are defeated. Now the woman, the eight kings and their client kings make war on the Lamb and are defeated. This theme will be repeated again in Rev 20:8 when Satan is released and gathers the Gog and Magog for a great battle, but are defeated. Satan is persistent and resilient but is constantly defeated. Finally, in the end, God will cast the beast (the Roman civil power), the false prophet (the Roman emperor cult) and Satan into the lake of fire which is the final judgment, and Satan and sin will be no more (Rev 20:10).

The Doom of Babylon is Announced - 18:1-24

In a striking way this block of material reveals how simple and easy it is for God to judge Babylon (Rome). John draws heavily on the symbolism of God's judgment of ancient Babylon which was prophesied and described so vividly in Isaiah and Jeremiah(cf. Isa 13;21:9; Jer 50 and 51). God's judgment on Babylon was so complete that the land had figuratively become a dwelling place for demons and every foul spirit. It became desolate and was stripped of its glory and wealth. Just so would be the extent of God's judgment on Rome. We must remember that Isaiah, Jeremiah, and John are speaking prophetically and symbolically, not merely historically. For John especially (but likewise for Isaiah and Jeremiah), the focus is not the eventual historical fall of the Roman Empire, but the extent and completeness of God's divine judgment of both Babylon and Rome.

This judgment is so easy for God that at first it is described as taking place in "a single day" (Rev 18:8). Then three times simply in one hour (Rev 18:10, 17, 19). As mighty as Rome might be, for God it is a simple matter to judge her and bring her to ruin. The nations symbolically marvel and mourn at the "demise" of Rome, for they had derived great wealth from their association with Rome. While the nations mourn for the demise of Rome, heaven, the saints, apostles, and prophets can rejoice in that God has judged Rome and vindicated his saints.

The section closes by clarifying that John is truly speaking symbolically of Rome, for in her as in Babylon "was found the blood of prophets and of saints, and of all who have been slain on earth" (18:24).

Summary of God's Authority over Rome

This section began by focusing attention on the seductive power of Rome and the Imperial cult. Rome was intoxicated by her power to seduce and destroy those who did not succumb to her seduction. As an evil beast that has a history of resilience, Rome would continue to persecute God's people, but as in the case of each of the emperors, all are consigned by God to perdition (ruin and destruction). They will make war on the saints and the Lamb, but the Lamb would defeat them.

Rome's judgment by God is certain. Furthermore, Rome's judgment is a simple matter for God, for he can achieved it in a single day, even in one hour! God's judgment is also so complete that Rome has no future glory left, it is reduced to absolute ruin.

1. Why does John refer to Rome as a harlot? What does that say about contemporary political powers?

2. What is the point of the seven kings who become an eighth and all go on to perdition? What contemporary lesson can we derive from this?

3. What lessons for daily life can we learn from the completeness and ease of God's judgment on Babylon/Rome?

4. Think about contemporary movies and books that depict themes of good over evil. What do you think this says about culture's view of the need to right wrongs? What differences do see in the way screenwriters and novelists communicate victory over evil and the way John says it will happen?

5. In Revelation God wins. Think and pray about what good news this is as we continue to struggle with evil in our lives and in the world. Share the news of God's victory with someone who feels the weight of evil in their lives. The message of Revelation can give comfort to those who suffer by leading them to depend on the one who will have final victory.

10

GOD'S TRUIMPH OVER EVIL

ROME WILL NOT STAND
REV 17:1-20:15
Part 2

Introduction

In this lesson we will discuss the final four descriptions of God's divine authority. We are reminded that God's judgment of Rome is a simple matter; he can accomplish it in one hour. Furthermore, his judgment and authority over Rome is absolute and complete. The section begins with praise to God for the marriage supper of the Lamb, and moves on through the defeat and judgment of the beast and the false prophet, to the binding and eventual defeat of Satan, the reign of the martyrs, and the final judgment.

The Marriage Super of the Lamb - 19:1-10

As in Revelation 4 and 15, heaven breaks out in songs of praise to God for his righteous judgments. He has answered the prayers of the saints (6:10 "how long...."). By his great power he has judged the harlot and "avenged on her the blood of his servants." He has exercised his sovereign reign over the earth. The Bride has made herself ready for the marriage to the Lamb. The image of the Bride should be seen in contrast to that of the harlot in Rev 17; Rome is typified as a harlot, the saints and martyrs as the Bride of the Lamb. John is obviously speaking symbolically and drawing on a common Hebrew concept of God being betrothed or wed to his people (Hos 2:19, Isa 54:5-7; 61:10, et al). Hebrew weddings were a drawn out experience which involved two events, sometimes separated by considerable time; a betrothal and the wedding. It is only after the wedding that the marriage is consummated. The analogy to that of the Christian and Christ is that in the present life the Christian is betrothed to Christ, the betrothal is to be consummated in heaven at the last day. A blessing pronounced on those invited to the wedding supper of the Lamb.

> *He was sternly warned not to worship the angel, for the angel is a fellow servant of God.*

John was so impressed by this scene that he fell down at the feet of the angel and worshipped him. He was sternly warned not to worship the angel, for the angel is a fellow servant of God. God alone is to be worshipped. The final sentence of 19:10,

"For the testimony of Jesus is the spirit of prophecy" is interesting, coming immediately after the command to worship God. The "testimony" refers to Jesus' death on the cross–it was a sacrificial death in reverence to God. Dying in reverence for God is what the spirit of prophecy is all about; God is worthy of all worship and sacrifice, even death. Dying as a martyr is the epitome of prophecy! Martyrdom is a statement about the believer and God; only God is worthy of worship, and the martyr is a faithful witness.

The Defeat of the Beast and False Prophet is Guaranteed - 19:11-21

The next scene depicts heaven opened and the crucified Jesus sitting on a white horse (19:13). He is the faithful and true (genuine) one! You can trust him! He (not Rome) is the one who rules over God's kingdom and judges all nations. He is King of kings and Lord of lords! In contrast to the wedding supper for the Bride and Lamb we now see another feast, that of the vultures! The contrast is striking! The vultures are invited to the feast of the beast and the false prophet, where they feast on the flesh of men, and from the context is seems, on the flesh of the beast and the false prophet. The sovereign Lamb captures the beast (Rome) and the false prophet (the emperor cult) and throws them into the lake of fire which is proleptically (experienced or received in advance) analogous to the final judgment. We assume also from 14:9-11 that those who worship the beast and receive its mark share in this judgment! We should be careful to understand that the picture is not of the final judgment but of the beast and the false prophet. They are immediately to experience the intensity of that last event in advance of the final judgment.

We are introduced here to an interesting phenomenon of biblical expression. Although the final judgment is not yet realized, God pronounces end of the world judgment on Rome and others before the actual final judgment occurs. We likewise today experience end of the world salvation in advance of the actual end of the world. Paul and Luke speak in terms of realized salvation; Peter speaks of a salvation still to be realized (1 Pet 1:3-9, et al). John speaks of eternal life already a reality (1 John 5:13 et al), and yet, still to be realized at the end of time.

The point here is that although we are reading of the judgment of the beast and the false prophet (Rome) we are not reading of the final judgment, only a proleptic (experienced or received in advance) expression of the final judgment! The purpose of this type of expression serves to drive home the certainty, reality, and in some sense, the finality of one's present actions and beliefs. Rome, because of her evil and refusal to repent, is already judged in the present with end of the world finality.

The Binding of Satan is Assured - 20:1-3; 7-10

This block of material has given rise to more speculation than possibly any other in the Bible! A major reason for this is that this text is so rich in symbolism. Commentators given to a literal interpretation have difficulty interpreting symbolism and figurative literature. Revelation 20:1-10 is aptly spoken of as the cradle of Millennial theology, especially Premillennialism and Dispensationalism. Both of these millennial theologies expect the earthly return of Christ before he establishes his kingdom (reign) on earth. We should point out in advance that the visions described in this block of material nowhere speak of a kingdom being established on earth, in fact the scenes depict cosmic or extraterrestrial phenomena.

For the sake of convenience when following the thrust of John's vision we should understand that 20:4-6 forms a parenthetical statement that can be read separately from the flow of thought being developed by John in 20:1-10. It is easy to see this as we connect 20:3 to 20:7. We will return to 20:4-6 shortly to insert this significant paragraph into the context of the passage.

20:1-2

   20:3 " ...threw him into the Abyss... until the thousand years ended."
    (20:4-6)
   20:7 " ...the thousand years are over, Satan will be released..."

20:8-10

The first scene (vv 1-3) depicts an angel who has authority over the bottomless pit (the abyss, a source of evil) and a great chain. He seizes the devil, binds him with the chain for a thousand years, throws him into the bottomless pit, and seals it. When the thousand years is ended, Satan is released to continue his evil deeds (v 7). He recruits Gog and Magog, who according to Hebrew tradition represent rebellious nations opposed to God. Satan again makes war on God's people with the same result, he is defeated, but this time completely and absolutely (8:10). The role of Gog and Magog in Hebrew tradition is interesting, for not only do they represent nations that are opposed to God, they also symbolize the resilience of evil.

Although the Old Testament says nothing about binding evil spirits with a chain, some Jewish literature in the Apocrypha and other Jewish writings make use of this metaphor on several occasions. The most notable is in Tobit 8 where Tobias remembers instructions an angel named Raphael, had given him to burn the liver of a certain fish in his house to repel an evil spirit. The evil spirit troubling him would flee into the desert where the angel would bind him. It seems apparent that this and similar legends lay behind the intriguing symbolism of the binding of Satan. The point of the symbolic binding of Satan is that his power to deceive the nations would be limited, which in the context of Revelation would refer to Rome and her client king nations. The scheme of redemption revealed in the scroll of Revelation 5 and 6 thus included God limiting or removing Satan's power to use Rome for his evil deeds of persecuting the church.

The figure of "one thousand years" is also intriguing. There are a few scattered instances of use of the term in scripture such as 2 Pet 3:8 and Ps 90:4, which express the idea that with the Lord one thousand years is like a day, and references in Psalms such as Ps 50:10 where the psalmist refers to cattle on a thousand hills belonging to the Lord. Eccl 6:6 speaks analogously of living for a thousand years. The Apocryphal book

Sirach (Ecclesiasticus) 41:4 records this interesting statement "Whether life is for ten or a hundred or a thousand years, there is no inquiry about it in Hades."

From these and similar statements scholars have concluded that one thousand, or ten cubed, symbolizes completeness. This would lead to the conclusion that Satan is ultimately and completely limited in his ability to deceive the nations (Rome and her client nations). The binding of Satan in this context implies that God will limit Satan's power to use Rome for his evil purposes.

But Satan is resilient! His resilience is well known from scripture. He is defeated by Jesus at Jesus' temptation, but continues to oppose Jesus and God's plan (Lk 4:1-13). Michael and his heavenly host defeat Satan in heaven, but Satan continues the battle on earth (Rev 12). In Revelation Satan is limited in regard to Rome (he is bound for a thousand years), but he returns in other situations (Gog and Magog) to take up the war against God's people. But he will again be defeated! Satan will finally be judged and defeated and thrown into the lake of fire (Rev 20:10) where he will be tormented day and night for ever and ever! This will fulfill God's plan.

Inserted into this intriguing discussion of the limitation of Satan's power to use Rome as his agent of evil is the challenging paragraph regarding the saints reigning for one thousand years. We should note first of all that this passage nowhere says that Christ will reign for one thousand years! And nowhere does it say that this thousand year reign will take place on earth! Christ reigns in his kingdom eternally! Dan 7:14, which is a foundational text for John in Revelation, speaks of the son of man receiving an eternal kingdom:

> And to him was given dominion and glory and kingdom, that all peoples, nations, and languages should serve him; his dominion is an everlasting dominion, which shall not pass away, and his kingdom one that shall not be destroyed.

In Rev 20:4-6 it is the martyrs (those who have been beheaded for their testimony to Jesus) who reign for on thousand years. The martyrs reign with Christ for a thousand years, but Christ reigns eternally. And this reign is in heaven not on earth! The symbolism of the martyrs reigning with Christ for one thousand years is that they reign completely or fully with Christ in his kingdom as the reward for their faithfulness unto death. This has been a recurring theme in Revelation (see 2:26, 27; 3:21). Although all Christians corporately reign with Christ in his kingdom, Revelation was written specifically to reassure the martyrs that death for the Christian is not defeat, but victory!

Revelation 20:5, 6 has posed significant problems for commentators of all persuasions! The consensus of most commentators who are not Dispensational or Premillennial is that the first resurrection symbolically refers to the death of the martyrs (their resurrection to reigning with Christ), and the second death to the final judgment. References relating to the "rest of the dead" either refer to all other persons not specifically addressed in Revelation, or to those who dwell on earth, that is, those opposed to God. It is most likely that Rev 20:5 is a parenthetical statement that could be read around.

The Final Judgment is Introduced - 20:11-15

As a closing statement to this section on the authority of God over evil and all creation, John includes a comment on the final end of the world judgment. Revelation is not really about the end of the world. It is about God's plan for handling the problem of evil, and especially Rome. But to round out the story and argument about the problem of evil one has to finalize the theodicy (defense of God in the face of evil) by "bringing the curtain down" on evil. Hence the final judgment is briefly, but significantly included in Revelation. In this section we return to the heavenly scene (Rev 4; 15) with the sovereign God on his throne opening the books of life and judgment. Satan has been judged and thrown into the lake of fire (20:10), now all of the dead, great and small, are judged in the final end of he world judgment. In the next section (21:1) we will see that the sea is no more! Evil no longer exists, for Satan has been judged and condemned to hell.

Summary of the Authority of God over Evil - Part 2

The second half of the major block which began in 17:1 and which stressed God's authority over all his creation, especially over evil, concludes in 20:15. This section began with the wedding supper of the Bride and the Lamb which reassured the martyrs of their place at the marriage feast of God and his people. This was followed by the defeat of the beast and the false prophet who were thrown into the lake of fire. Then Satan was seen bound and limited in his power to use Rome as his agent, only to be released to continue his evil work. Satan again gathered the nations for battle against God's people, but finally in God's plan and purpose Satan is defeated and thrown into the lake of fire along with the beast and the false prophet. The martyrs are depicted as reigning fully with Christ for one thousand years and so are reassured of their complete victory and reign with Christ in his Messianic kingdom. Finally, the curtain is brought down on God's plan of redemption for his creation. The final judgment is briefly presented, "the books" are opened, and all of the dead are judged by the Almighty God.

❧ Reflection and Application

1. What purpose does this section play in the overall theme and structure of Revelation? See 20:4-6.

2. Why the need to demonstrate that God ultimately has all authority?

3. Why was it necessary for Satan to be depicted as bound with a chain? What meaning did this have for the Christians of the 1st century? What significance does this have for Christians today?

4. What does it mean that Satan will be loosed again? What do Gog and Magog symbolize? What relevance does this have for our contemporary world? What is the final message to be learned from this analogy?

A Closer Look

In this section we have made reference to dispensational views such as Premillennialism and Dispensationalism. These views, which are somewhat related, hold that God has not yet established his Messianic kingdom. These views place the second coming of Christ before (pre-) the establishment of the messianic kingdom. Dispensationalism bases this on the rejection of Jesus by the Jews and holds to a postponed kingdom. Premillennialsim argues that the messianic kingdom promised to Israel was not fulfilled and still awaits fulfillment in Jerusalem. Both of these views take the rich symbolism of the 1000 years literally rather than symbolically. A third millennial view, Postmillennialism, places the second coming of Christ after (post-) the establishment of the messianic kingdom. Postmillennialism has in recent years lost popularity due to the fact that it is argued more along sociological than biblical lines. The view adopted in this study is commonly known as Amillennialism. Amillennialism seeks to maintain the figurative symbolism of Revelation, especially in regard to such figures as the beast and the 1000 years. As noticed above, Amillennialism identifies the 1000 years as a figure of completeness, the martyrs reign with Christ symbolically for 1000 years, or more correctly, they already reign completely with Christ. Satan is figuratively bound for 1000 years, meaning he is completely bound in regard to his ability to continue to use Rome as his agent. God has limited Satan's ability. Because Amillennialism is neither pre- or post-, but symbolic in its views of the 1000 years, it is identified as not (a-) millennial.

11
GOD'S CHURCH MADE PERFECT

DESCRIPTIONS OF THE NEW HEAVEN AND THE NEW EARTH
REV 21:1-22:5

Introduction

In Revelation 2 and 3 we saw Jesus addressing seven letters to the seven churches in Asia. We depicted this in our structural analysis of Revelation as Point I, representing The Church in Imperfection in which Jesus saw imperfection in five of his churches that needed correction. In John's chiastic structure (see lesson 1) this was balanced by Point VII, The Church in Perfection in which we see the perfected church in heaven. The intention of this section is to encourage the saints to see the true glory of the church in heaven in contrast to the struggles and extreme difficulty they were experiencing. We also see the glory of heaven contrasted with the corruption of this world and its world powers. Christians need to have a vision of hope on which to fix their attention as they struggle through life's difficulties. Read Rom 8:18-39 as a foundation for this study.

The New Heaven and New Earth - 21:1-8

John draws on the imagery of Isa 65:17 and 66:22 where in the restoration of Israel God promised a new heaven and new earth. The new in contrast to the old implies an antithesis, the new will be a new system, a new creation, a new age totally different from the old. For the old has passed away. This expression is common to the apocalyptic literature of Israel (1 Enoch 45:4-5, 72:1; 91:16; 2 Esdras 7:75; et al) expressing the promise and hope of a new world in which God himself reigned. We see this also in a similar context in 2 Pet 3:13. In this new world the sea (as an Hebrew idiom for a source of evil) is no more, implying that evil no longer exists for Satan has been judged and cast into the lake of fire. In this new creation there will be no more suffering, weeping and death, for these have been abolished together with evil. In this new existence God himself will dwell with the saints. This existence forms the promise to those who conquer (Rev 21:7), and no one who commits the lie of proclaiming that Caesar is Lord will have a place here, for their place is the lake of fire which is the second death (21:8). Notice how severe John is in defining those who worship the emperor. They are liars, cowards faithless, fornicators,

> *Christians need to have a vision of hope on which to fix their attention as they struggle through life's difficulties*

murderers, sorcerers, and idolaters! Notice also the contrast of the existence of the conquerors and those who worship the emperor! The new heaven where God dwells versus the lake of fire where Satan dwells!

The New Jerusalem - 21:9-22:5
John follows the description of the new heaven with a description of the new Jerusalem. The connection between Isa 65 and 66 and Rev 21 is not one of prophesy and fulfillment as some Premillennialists believe. Scripture employs several different types of fulfillment; typological fulfillment where, for example, Jesus is a type of Adam (Rom 5:12ff), analogous or allegorical fulfillment where the Christianity is analogous to or allegorically Sarah and the Law to Hagar (Gal 4:21ff); historical fulfillment where some historical event fulfills a prophecy of the past (Matt 2:6); Midrashic fulfillment where a new event has spiritual similarities to a previous event (Matt 2:17,18). The connection between Rev 21 and Isa 65 and 66 is a typological fulfillment where similar conditions exist. As Israel looked for a new home, a new heaven and earth, a new Jerusalem, so do Christians undergoing severe persecution and experiencing great suffering. The look for a new home in heaven with God, a new system, a new heavenly Jerusalem.

The Gates and Foundations of the City - 21:9-14
In this paragraph John draws on Ezek 40 and 48 in an analogous comparison, and not an historical fulfillment, as he describes the city. It has 12 gates inscribed with the names of the twelve tribes of Israel, three on each side, and twelve foundations inscribed with the names of the twelve apostles. The total of 24 (representing God's people from all ages) is similar to that in Rev 4 where 24 elders represent the martyrs of both Israel and the church. Here the new Jerusalem is not simply the city of Israel, but of all of God's people. It is not the earthly Jerusalem being described, but a heavenly Jerusalem (21:10).

The Measurements of the City - Rev 21:15-21
Again in an analogous comparison to Ezek 40 the heavenly Jerusalem is measured, signifying that this city is fully known by God, for it is his city. The city is enormous and magnificent, adorned by the most precious jewels. This figurative fact alone, the adornment of the city with precious jewels, signifies that John is speaking symbolically as he describes the glory of this city. The equivalent measurement as 12,000 stadia cubed would be approximately 1500 miles by 1500 miles by 1500 miles! Rome was a large magnificent city but even Rome pales in comparison to the new Jerusalem, the heavenly city of God. Augustine (ca 400 AD) drew on this contrast in his City of God as he set the City of God against the secular world and its efforts which one could identify with Rome.

> *Temples venerate a God who is absent or not visibly present to the worshippers.*

The Glory and Light of this City - 21:22-27

There is no need for a temple in this city! Temples venerate a God who is absent or not visibly present to the worshippers. Most of the cities to which Jesus addressed Revelation had magnificent temples to gods who were not there! Even Jerusalem had a temple to the God who dwelt in heaven. In this city there is no temple! There is no need for a temple, for God himself is present in this city! The almighty God himself is the temple of this city. Neither are there lights in this city, for the city reflects the light and glory of God himself. The great temple to Artemis in Ephesus shaped the life of Ephesus, and in some measure shaped the glory of Ephesus, but as we know, the temple to Artemis was destroyed and slipped into oblivion. Pergamum was resplendent with temples to the Roman gods and even the great temple to Aesclepius would eventually pass into ruin. But the city of God is shaped by the presence of God almighty and reflects his glory and light. The light of this city never goes out and provides safety for all. Again, John reminds the reader that no falsehood or anything unclean may enter this city, only those whose names are written in the lamb's book of life. In the context of Revelation this means that no-one who has worshipped the beast and thus committed falsehood has a place in this city, for it is reserved for those who are faithful.

The Sustenance of this City - 22:1-5

We have already noticed that those who conquer will eat of the tree of life which is in the paradise of God, and live forever (2:7). They will also eat of the spiritual food of hidden manna, and receive an invitation to the eschatological (end of the world) banquet with God (3:17). John resumes this theme by explaining that in this city are both the river and tree of life which provide "year round" food. Nothing accursed is to be found in this city (this excludes those who have worshipped the beast), for in this city are the throne of God and the Lamb who reign eternally in the presence of their people who worship them for ever and ever. Only those who bear the name of God on their forehead (that is, the conquerors - others bear the mark of the beast) are found in this city. Other parts of scripture promise that all of God's faithful servants will be there, but in this passage, John's focus is on the conquerors who bear the name of God and the Lamb on their foreheads. His intent is to reassure those facing martyrdom that their place in this city is secure.

Summary of the Vision of the Heavenly City, the New Jerusalem

These visions of the new Jerusalem coming down out of heaven are intended to serve two purposes. First, they are set in contrast to the seven imperfect churches described Rev 2 and 3. Here we see the church in its heavenly state in the very presence of God, rather than with its human imperfection and weaknesses. Second, the new heavenly Jerusalem, the city of God, is set in contrast with the cities of this world symbolized by Rome. Those who share in the city of this world have no place in the city of God!

To reassure those facing martyrdom, and to encourage them not to compromise their faith in any manner with either the world or the emperor cult, John repeatedly points out that nothing unclean or faithless, no one guilty of falsehood (worshipping the beast) will be able to enter this city.

ᔧ Reflection and Application

1. What is the connection between Ezek 40, Isa 65 and 66, and this passage discussing the new heaven and new earth in Revelation?

2. What role do these visions of the new Jerusalem, the city of God, play in the context of Revelation?

3. What reasons could one give for not perceiving the new Jerusalem to be a physically or historically restored Jerusalem in Israel or Palestine?

4. Americans seem to have considerable interest in science fiction. Movies, cartoons, books, and magazines betray a certain disallusionment with the world as it is and focus on themes of destruction of the earth. What does John's vision of the new heaven and the new earth have to say to this culture?

A Closer Look

In this chapter we have drawn attention to the fact that the style of "fulfillment" encountered in highly symbolic literature as in Revelation is different from what is normally viewed as prophecy and fulfillment. This fits in well with the nuanced difference between normal Prophecy and Apocalyptic Prophecy. Normal Prophecy and Fulfillment sees the fulfillment a literal historical fulfillment of a prophetic utterance. We might see such a connection in the prophecy of Jesus (Matt 24) that Jerusalem will be destroyed. This occurred in AD 70 when the Romans laid siege to Jerusalem and destroyed it completely. However, several other types of "fulfillment" are encountered in Scripture. There are Typological or Analogous types of fulfillment where the prophet draws on a previous prophetic utterance and fulfillment and draws a parallel to this in a form of fulfillment where the new prophecy is a similar type of occasion. The prophet may also be making an analogous comparison to a previous prophetic utterance and fulfillment. We encounter this type of "prophecy and fulfillment" in Revelation which is full of figurative expressions. Here the prophet draws attention to the fact that the new prophetic utterance is similar or analogous to some previous occasion. In the case of Revelation John draws on Isaiah and Jeremiah and their prophetic utterances regarding Babylon which were historically fulfilled. When

John uses this language he is not intending that the fulfillment of his prophetic utterance is a second fulfillment of the previous Old Testament prophecy regarding Babylon. His intention is that his prophecy and its fulfillment are similar, or analogous to the previous prophecy and fulfillment. He is not connecting his prophecy to the previous prophecies in Isaiah or Jeremiah as a second fulfillment. We have also mentioned a Midrashic fulfillment in which a later writer uses a previous prophetic utterance and finds new meaning in this, also in an analogous manner. We do not encounter this form of prophecy in Revelation, but it is found at least ten times in Matthew's Gospel. This Midrashic type of expression is significantly Jewish in nature and was clearly understood by Jewish believers.

12

THE EPILOGUE

REV 22:6-21

Introduction

In the unique chiastic structure of Revelation John has balanced or offset a Prologue (Rev 1:1-20) with an Epilogue (Rev 22:6-21) in which he repeats several of the significant themes introduced in the Prologue. This literary technique was common in ancient writings and served to emphasize the main themes of the work as though the Prologue and Epilogue were two bookends holding the meaning or theology of the work together. Technically we can also call this an inclusio in that it includes and sets boundaries for the significant thoughts of the writing in a unified theme.

Themes and Statements of the Prologue - 1:1-20

For the sake of convenience we list the salient themes and statements, or theological emphases of the Prologue:

1. The revelation comes from the eternal God, his Son, and the Holy Spirit (1:1-6)
2. The revelation was communicated through angels to God's servants (1:1)
3. The revelation concerned things that must soon take place (1:1-3)
4. The time is near (1:3)
5. A blessing is pronounced on those who keep the message of the prophecy (1:1-3)
6. The message and visions are so striking that John falls down to worship (1:17)
7. The message of revelation is from Jesus for the churches (1:11)
8. God is the alpha and omega (1:8)
9. Jesus is the first and the last (1:17)
10. Jesus is the one who comes in judgment (1:7)

Themes and Statements in the Epilogue Common to the Prologue - 22:6-21

We list the common themes in the same order as they appear in the Prologue:

1. The revelation comes from the eternal God (22:6)
2. The revelation was communicated through angels (22:6)
3. The revelation concerned things that must soon take place (22:6)
4. The time is near (Rev 22:10)

5. A blessing is pronounced on those who keep the message of the prophecy (22:7) (In the Epilogue a warning is added to the blessing – 22:18)

6. The message and visions are so striking that John falls down to worship, this time to worship and angel but is warned by the angel to worship only God (22:8)

7. The message of revelation is from Jesus for the churches (22:16)

8. Jesus is the alpha and omega (22:13)

9. Jesus is the first and the last (22:13)

10. Jesus is coming in judgment (22:12)

The Message of the Epilogue in Detail – 2:6-21

The Epilogue begins with Jesus reminding the churches that he is trustworthy and true. The implication is that he can be relied on in regard to several matters. He has himself experienced martyrdom and knows from personal experience that God will raise the martyr. "I am...the living one; I died, and behold I am alive for evermore..." (1:18). He has proven his right through his own martyrdom to expect extreme faith and commitment from his followers. He had warned his disciples that persecution and martyrdom would in many cases accompany discipleship (Matt 10:16-39; 16:24-28). Jesus closes the revelation by stressing the urgency of his message and the need for the saints to heed the warnings. He again calls for uncompromising faith, "for the time is near" (22:10). He reassures his saints that he has heard their cries for vindication and promises "I am coming soon, bringing my recompense" (22:12). The statement that he is coming soon should not be interpreted as a reference to his second coming, but to his coming in the context of the trials and need of the churches in Asia. He is already constantly present in the life of the churches (he is the one walking around in the midst of the lampstands – 2:1). He will bring imminent judgment on those individuals and churches who do not repent, and he will remove their lampstand, that is their right to be a church (2:5). He is coming in judgment on the beast and the false prophet (Rome) and will judge them with end of the world consequences. All of this he will do before the final end of the world, or his second coming. It is a fallacy to believe that Jesus is not already active in his kingdom and church, and reigning in the world; that he is sitting idly and helplessly by as his church suffers! He promises the churches in Asia that he is coming soon bringing his recompense on those who dishonor them and him (those who dwell on earth or who worship the beast).

Jesus again promises a blessing on those who wash their robes (die as martyrs). They have the right to the tree of life (2:7; 22:2; 22:14). In keeping with his predilection for grouping things in sevens (heptets), we have in 22:14 the last of seven blessings in Revelation (1:3; 14:13; 16:15; 19:9; 20:6; 22:7; and 22:14). The concept of blessedness derives from Hebrew roots and implies a spiritual condition of being spiritually rich. It does not mean "happy" as some would contend, but as in the Beatitudes of Matt 5 speaks of a spiritual confidence and tranquility that derives from the knowledge that God favors the blessed ones in spite of trials and hardship. The martyrs are blessed by their presence in the city of God. Outside this blessed city, in the city of the world, that is in the context of Revelation, Rome, are the dogs (unclean ones) sorcerers, fornicators, and everyone who practices falsehood (worships the beast).

Those facing martyrdom receive an invitation directly from Jesus, the son of David, (the one who reflects the glory of divine Messiahship – the morning star) to come and share the blessings of the spiritual water of life without price. This is similar to the invitation to the eschatological (end of the world) banquet received by the conqueror in the letter to Pergamum (the little white stone of 2:17). Jewish and Christian tradition reflects a pervasive expectation of a great banquet at the end of the world when all the redeemed will sit at the table of the Lord and enjoy the riches of his heavenly provision (Ps 23 and the Lord's Supper [or communion] reflect this expectation). Jesus repeats his invitation to the martyrs to this banquet with these encouraging words "The Spirit and the Bride say, 'Come.' And let him who hears say, 'Come.' And let him who is thirsty come, let him who desires take the water of life without price."

Following this invitation, however, Jesus issues a stern warning that should anyone add to or take away words from the prophecy of Revelation (that is compromise their faith) God would deny them their share in the tree of life and the city of God. There will always be those who will not take seriously God's warnings to be prepared for the challenges brought to the Christian by the repeated and devious activity of Satan. We should be careful to limit our interpretation of this warning not to "add to nor take away" from the words of this prophecy. This warning is strengthened when it is seen in context of the seriousness of Revelation. There are other similar passages in which Moses and others have warned against adding to God's word. Each of these statements must be understood within the context of their message. To bind such statements as universal prohibitions without limiting them to their context does an injustice to sound hermeneutics (biblical interpretation). Literalists fall prey to this tendency.

Compromise with the world is an ever present reality the Christian must engage and resist. In Revelation, the reader is called to resist compromise with Satan. We know from church history, especially from the era which we are engaging in Revelation, that compromise with the Imperial Cult was tempting and attractive, and many Christians fell into this trap, creating real problems for the church after the persecution ended. How does the church, or should the church accept back into fellowship those members who have compromised their faith with the Imperial Cult? The church faces similar challenges today. When Christians compromise their faith with the world, it is "almost impossible" (the writer of Hebrews says it is impossible! – Heb 6:4) to restore them to faith again.

Jesus closes his message by again reassuring the churches that he is coming soon to take care of their concerns and to answer their prayers and cries for vindication (6:10). John adds the benedictory prayer that the grace (favor) of the Lord Jesus be with all the saints.

Summary of the Epilogue – 22:6-21
In many cases the Epilogue "shadows" the Prologue, echoing the urgency of the

message concerning the imminence and certainty of a crisis soon to come on the church in Asia, and calling on the churches to hear the call of God to an uncompromising faith. The Epilogue, like the Prologue reminds the church that the message of Revelation comes directly from the almighty God and his Son, Jesus. The Epilogue adds a reassuring invitation to the banquet in the city of God, and warns the church not to weaken God's call to unyielding faithfulness to Jesus and God. The Epilogue also adds a reassuring note that Jesus would vindicate and avenge his saints.

❧ Reflection and Application

1. What role do the Prologue and Epilogue play in Revelation? Why do you think it was necessary for John to include the emphases we find in the Prologue and Epilogue?

2. If the historical setting of the crises and judgments of Revelation are the 1st century church in Asia, what significance do the emphases of the Prologue and Epilogue have for the church today?

3. John issues a strong warning to remain faithful. What issues or situations threaten to weaken your commitment? Sometimes we describe unfaithfulness in terms of blatant disregard for the ways of Christ or in terms of having different opinions and understandings of scripture. Are there other forms of unfaithfulness?

4. Physical challenges can become spiritual challenges. When we hurt or suffer the distresses of this life it is tempting to look in the wrong place for relief or comfort. How is the picture of Jesus as one who suffered helpful in these circumstances?

SOME ADVANCED READING
FOR REVELATION

The following is a short list of good research tools in the study of Revelation.

G. B. Caird, *The Revelation of Saint John the Divine*, Harper and Row, 1966
  (Intermediate)

Robert Mounce, *The Book of Revelation*, Eerdmans, 1997 (Intermediate)

Colin Hemer, *The Letters to the Seven Churches of Asia in their Local Setting*,
  The University of Sheffield, England, 1986
  (Comprehensive. The best on the seven cities)

G. K. Beale, *The Book of Revelation*, Eerdmans, 1999 (Advanced, technical)

M. Eugene Boring, *Revelation*, Interpretation, John Knox, 1989 (For preachers)